Nature's

Celebrating the Seasons in a Pagan Family

by Rachel Mayatt

www.capallbann.co.uk

Nature's Children

ISBN 186163 285 1
ISBN 13 9781861632852

Cover design by HR Design
Cover and internal illustrations by Rachel Mayatt

Published by:

Capall Bann Publishing
Auton Farm
Milverton
Somerset
TA4 1NE

This book is dedicated to all my Teachers I have been fortunate enough to have worked with. To all my friends, students and other magickal colleagues.

And finally - especially to my children - Richard, Julia and Rhiannon, who were the inspiration for this work.

Contents

Introduction

I have written this book because there seems to be few books on seasonal celebrations that include your children. Indeed most books with instruction on craft activities, Pagan circles and ritual whether Wiccan, Druidic or any other tradition tends to focus on adults without looking at the family aspect of Paganism. There are one or two that may touch on this briefly, or have ideas to celebrate the seasons that can be used with children as well as adults, and I mention some of these in further references.

I am an experienced third degree Wiccan of over 20 years experience, having run groups and taught workshops all over the South East of England, and I am a Mother of three children so I think I can claim to write with some authority on this subject. My older children - Richard and Julia are now adults and the youngest - Rhiannon is 3 years old. I brought up my older two children with a sympathetic but non-Pagan ex-partner which meant I was only able to show them a partial Pagan/Wiccan way of life.

This is not the case with my youngest, which enables me to do things a little differently - raising her in a completely Pagan family environment. However, at the end of the day it is important to remember; as in any magical activity (and raising a child is indeed a magical act!) it is always the intention that is most important. My motivation is that I think my way of life is a good one, and I would like my children to appreciate and respect the Earth, which is their home. Like most mothers I have made mistakes as well as successes, but I believe I've always had good motives behind my actions. This is certainly not the only way to raise a Pagan child, but it is how I am doing it at the moment.

I have organised this book in a yearly format, following the seasons and the eight major festivals of the year. I want to show how I include children in celebrating Pagan life. Many of my group members have families too and so their children are always welcome to join our festival celebrations too. Within that context I realise that there will be differences in the ages of the children. So although I am writing this mainly for families with younger children - not yet in their teens, older children may also enjoy doing the activities aimed at their younger siblings and I don't think it's hard to adapt things where necessary. I have included ideas to introduce the moon phases and other aspects of Pagan living - teaching about the elements, the Goddess and God etc.

I also feel it important to look at the wider aspects bringing up a child in a Pagan household - education, socialisation and outside effects on the family. Finally I have ideas for rites of passage, such as celebrating birth of children, birthdays, coming of age for boys and girls (particularly for girls for when they first start menstruation), and dealing with death.

I have not included things like handfasting or croning as these are not particularly relevant to this work, although children may take part in the rites to celebrate them both. At the end I have listed some useful and supportive organisations.

To use this book I would suggest you read through it and pick out ideas and suggestions you like that would fit your family situation, or use it to work out your own. Whether you find the majority of this book useful, or just some ideas that may prompt further ones, I hope it inspires you and you find it as rewarding to raise your children as I have.

Chapter One

SPRING

Imbolg   Spring Equinox

I always felt it was important to be creative in my spiritual beliefs. Not just to acknowledge the festivals, but to truly put the craft into the Craft. One of the things I was taught and teach my adult students is to try and make as many working tools, incenses and spell ingredients as I can. Putting the effort into creating something and making a link of energy between me and the item is part of the magical act. It's also fun! I want to impart this fun to my children and so we make things to hang in the home for different times of the year, or to symbolise something to do with each season. This also gives us a real sense of the changes of the cycles of the year, and of our lives. Creating the connection to our natural world.

Imbolg

Imbolg is the first festival of the spring, although it really is very early spring. The earth is still hard from frost - there may still be snow around, and it may seem like winter is never going to end. Under the Earth though it is a different matter. New shoots are slowly birthing, energy is stirring.

It is lovely to have rituals and celebrations outside when weather permits, but its not always possible if you don't have access to a garden or private grounds anywhere. I used to have the benefit of using a friends farmland for outdoor ritual in the past, but as its not possible these days, what I like to do is make sure we have an outing in the countryside, by the sea or at least in a nearby park as a prelude to any family celebrations. We may have had several previous outings to gather things to use for the actual ceremony such as leaves or acorns too.

So for the festival of Imbolg we collect any early greenery available to decorate the altar but please don't pick any early wild flowers as they are protected. Rhiannon is at a lovely stage at the moment where she spontaneously cuddles the trees on our woodland walks, and I feel a ramble out clears the winter cobwebs and helps us feel connected to the Goddess. So its wellies on, and out we go. I will chat about the time of year and what Imbolg means while we walk.

Sometimes we have other Pagan friends and their children too. We usually have a picnic and find a sheltered spot to stop and share a lunch together. I also make a point of bringing some extra food. We will have made bird seed balls to hang off a branch of a tree. We might leave some stale bread out for the birds, and we will leave a food offering for the spirits of the land. You might want to talk about the faery folk or if you work in Shamanism you could talk about the animal and tree spirits.

Before our trip, we may gather some seeds and bless them asking them to represent something we want to grow in our lives. Then we will plant them in the wild on our walk. If we're walking by the sea, we may take a couple of pebbles, draw a symbol to represent our requests and then throw them in the sea. I would also explain what the elements do and why we ask them to help us. Earth for our food and physical home, Water for our feelings and dreams when we sleep, Fire to give us energy to play and do, and Air to help us think and have ideas.

We will have other activities leading up to the day of the festival too. I like to keep an eye out for local fairs and customs so that we can go along and join in. There may be a local well dressing or early spring fayre. We like to make Imbolg cards to send to our Pagan friends, and we make up seasonal blessings and songs. We have started a family book. It is an album with cards, photos and our personal blessings and songs for the seasons. It's a lovely thing to do and it keeps growing because there are always new ideas to add. You may like to do something similar. It's a bit like a book of shadows for the family and children. We often paint or draw pictures to do with the festival - perhaps a triple goddess or a well dressed with flowers to hang over the altar, or make something with modelling clay. In a way we are creating our own Hereditary tradition of the Craft.

If you have a garden, it is best to get your children out and hands in the earth as young as they can. This is the time to get out and clear any weeds you didn't manage to deal with last autumn, to get ready for spring planting. If it's possible, give the children their own patch to grow what they want (with your help of course). If like me, you don't have a garden (I have a balcony), find out if there are allotments locally to grow as much of your own vegetables and flowers as you can. You can always share one with another family to lessen the hard work and they're really cheap to rent - about £20 a year. Put pots on your balcony or in the home and plant seeds with the children. I have several large tubs with herbs growing and hanging baskets to plant strawberry plants in when the frosts finish. Luckily I am fortunate that my balcony faces woodland where we observe foxes and squirrels on every day!

The day of the festival for our family celebration, we have a proper cast Wiccan circle in the tradition in which I was trained, although you may prefer something more simple. The altar is decorated with the greenery we collected, or pebbles from the beach, driftwood and anything else picked up. Before-hand, we make Well-shaped cheesy pastry or the triple Goddess symbol of a circle with two half circles either side- Imbolg is a celebration of the triple goddess Brighid (also known as Bride), who governs healing and wells among other things. The chalice is filled with fruit juice - obviously wine is not suitable for young children.

Although young children shouldn't handle the candles and incense, you can still use them if there are sufficient adults to watch the children whilst the circle is being cast, or you could swap them with something else to represent the elements of air and fire. Personally, I prefer to keep the candles and incense - but put up where the children can't touch them. I want the children to feel included though, so after blessing the water and salt, I usually ask them to sprinkle the circle boundary (with supervision). Other tasks can be assigned to them too - such as ringing the altar bell if you use one and passing around the chalice and bread or cakes.

Remember that although it is etiquette for group members/ guests to stay in the circle once it is cast, young children often move in and out of its boundaries. This is fine - animals and children are seen as innocent and will not break the circle bounds. If it's a family gathering, then I ask guests to leave their athames out of the circle - knives have no place around young children. A wand you have made together is a lovely thing for them to handle and they soon learn to draw an invoking pentagram at each direction.

After the opening and welcoming the Goddess, we will have a story. Brighid is often depicted with a spinning wheel -

14

which spins the thread of life and death. We usually have a story with a spinning wheel such as sleeping beauty. This can be used to symbolise the spring sleeping waiting for the prince (the God) to wake her. Afterwards we will make Brighid dolls. These will be hung up in the home - one of them as the family doll will be hung with her 'husband' (the corn dolly we made last year).

Next we will probably have a spiral dance. We may bring some musical instruments and drums into the circle, or make some shakers with boxes and seeds or lentils before-hand. Family and guests blessings and requests/prayers follow the dance.

Finally the pastry shapes and fruit juice are blessed and shared before the circle is closed. As always, we ask any guests to bring food to share after the celebration ends. Then tired little children are off to bed and hopefully dream of the spring while the adults have a chalice of wine or two!

Making the items for the Festival

Bird Seed Balls

Take equal amounts of mixed bird seed (wild bird seed is available from pet shops)

Stale bread and lard or dripping. Melt the dripping in a saucepan and mix the seed and bread until it is soaking with the fat. Put into empty yogurt pots or pie cases. Put into the fridge to cool. When cold and firm remove from pots and tie string around them. Keep cold until you take them outside to tie from tree branches.

Cheesy pastry wells and triple goddess symbols

Take a pack of pastry (or make your own - even better) and roll out

Grate mature cheddar cheese and sprinkle half onto pastry. Fold and roll out again.

Sprinkle the rest of the cheese and press gently. Season with salt and pepper.

Cut out well shapes or triple goddess moon shapes.

Baste with beaten egg yolk or milk and bake for about 10 minutes in a moderate oven. Leave to cool.

Brighid Dolls

Collect an assortment of material scraps, sequins, feathers, ribbon, wool etc. Felt tip pens PVC glue and a small wooden spoon.

Draw a face on the wooden spoon bowl and glue wool on for hair. Cut material out in the shape of a dress and tie or glue onto the handle of the spoon. Decorate as you wish.

Children's Wand

On one of your woodland walks look out for a small branch of any wood you prefer. Let your child choose as its going to be used by her. Ask your child to warn the tree you intend to cut a piece of branch. Cut a piece about the size of her arm from elbow to finger tip. Remember to tell your child to thank the tree afterwards.

The action of always telling a living thing of your intentions and thanking it afterwards is a good thing to teach a child from an early age. It helps them to realise they are part of a greater thing rather than just an individual. I believe it helps promote more connection for them with their natural surroundings, and of course, a respect for nature.

Allow the branch to dry out for a few weeks in an airing cupboard or other warm place. Your child can paint it or decorate it anyway she wishes. Perhaps you can spell out her name in runes along one side. I would fasten a quartz crystal on the end and varnish to finish.

Eostara - Spring Equinox

The weather should be a lot brighter and warmer now although there can still be the odd snow flurry here and there. The days are longer and the evenings lighter. Our clocks will be put forward an hour as we 'spring forward'. This is the height of spring activity under the earth and the blossoms will have started to bloom, leaves are showing on the trees, and daffodils and other spring flowers should be well and truly out. Animals are mating and birds are out nesting in the trees opposite my window. The festival comes from the Saxon Goddess Eostre and has been overtaken by the christians to become Easter - although that celebration moves from year to year depending on the moon tides. Mothering Sunday may also be around this time. The Easter symbols of Eggs and rabbits (traditionally hares) are previous Pagan symbols representing fertility and life. The egg is twice born - first when laid, and second when it hatches so has a mystical fertility connection.

The equinox is also a time of balance, day and night in equal length and the days will become longer moving on towards their height at the summer solstice. Snakes are also associated with Eostara - shedding its skin is symbolic of death and rebirth and also represents the earth energy - serpent lines (ley lines). The Hare is an animal of the Goddess. In earlier times it was forbidden to hunt and kill the hare and the manic behaviour of the mad-march hare was seen as sacred - a reference to the mentally ill who were believed to have been touched by the Gods.

As with Imbolg, our celebrations will probably start before the actual festival with outings to collect any things for the altar or craft making. On some of our walks in the countryside I will collect nettles to make nettle wine, soup or dry for nettle tea. Although I always teach my children not to touch plants they don't know and will always supervise them on our country foraging, I think its important they realise they can find nourishment from nature and not all food comes from the supermarket!! Once again I look out for any local festivals or interesting places to visit. Its lovely to visit a farm when lambing is taking place, piglets are suckling and the young animals can be seen. Near my home is a rare-breed centre open to the public, and we have been fortunate to watch the lambs being born and then stroke some of the 3 day old lambs - a real treat for young children and again, getting in touch with the nature of the season.

I also like to make a trip to the sea at this time with a picnic and any company that wants to come along too. We scavenge the beach for driftwood, holey stones and interesting shells. I like to look for small regular shaped pebbles about a centimetre round to make small sets of Futhark or witches runes as gifts. We may make the driftwood into mobiles with shells and feathers to hang in our home - asking for a blessing from the sea. The children make mandalas with shells and sand swirls to put on the wall above the altar. I tell them the mandalas help us to daydream/meditate. If you know anyone who keeps snakes you can ask them to give you a shed skin to put on the altar or wrap around another wand to use for Eostara or as a gift for a friend. Hanging in the window we make large sun wheels to catch the sunlight which dances on our walls. We may make cards again to send to our Pagan friends and will create our family songs specially for this time of balance. As well as putting fresh flowers on the altar, the children like to make some out of card and tissue paper - usually daffodils or tulips.

It's easy to get egg moulds to make your own chocolate eggs or buy plain hollow eggs you can decorate with icing piped with pentagrams or the sun wheel rune and other symbols of your choice. We also make cakes and decorate with nests full of eggs for the altar, and lay large round cheeses to represent the sun.

The gathering begins in the same way as before, a traditional circle with invitation to the Goddess as usual. I may have boiled and decorated some eggs earlier and hidden them in our home for the children to hunt out later. Of course if you have a garden, you can hide some eggs for the children to hunt after the circle is closed if its not too late, or for the next morning if the light has gone. After the circle is cast we may have a story about peter rabbit or the tortoise and the hare. It may be the ugly duckling - a very loose egg connection I know, but it is a story about transformation!! Then we will sing our songs or family blessings inviting our guests to join in.

Sometime beforehand I will have blown eggs and dried the hollow shells. We will decorate the egg and write a wish for us, a wish for a friend and one for the world to insert in the hole at the top. Although understanding the concept of 'world peace' is not possible for a 3 year old, teaching them to wish their toddler group has a happy easter holiday or some such desire is easier for them to grasp. As they get older the wish can be more mature in nature. It is important because they are learning from an early age to consider others as well as themselves.

We will follow with a dance - possible a circle dance and with Rhiannon and her friends it is expected that a rendition or two of 'hop little bunnies' will be required! Finally the cakes and juice will be blessed and shared, the circle closed and food shared before the children retire to hunt for eggs or go to bed if its late.

Making the items for the Festival

Sea stone rune sets

Collect 24 even shaped pebbles and inscribe the Futhark symbols on each one with a silver or gold pen. Put a dab of varnish over the top when the ink has dried. Make a small pouch with a drawstring to put them in. You can use the witches' runes instead if you like to use them. Older children like to make these too.

Sponge cake egg nests

Using a recipe for simple sponge cakes, when cool, slice the top off the sponges to make them flat and ice them with chocolate icing. Caramelise some sugar in water and dribble on the top in circular movements. It will look like sugar twig nests. When cool add 2 or 3 little solid chocolate eggs.

Egg shell spell

Blow several eggs to leave empty shells. Rinse the inside and leave to dry. Using glue, glitter, pens, paint, feathers ribbon etc decorate the eggs. Write a sentence on scrap paper to represent your wishes - i.e. Fresh Water For Drought Victims In Ethiopia. Taking the first letter of each word, write the new word on a small piece of parchment -

FWFDVIE

Roll up the parchment and slip into the egg through the hole in the shell. Hang the decorated egg in your home until Beltane and then smash it to release your wish.

Songs

Hop Little Bunnies
(all children lie on the floor 'sleeping')
See the sleeping Bunnies - sleeping unto noon
Shall we wake them, with a merry tune.
See how still. Are they Ill?   No - WAKE UP!
(children get up and jump about)
Hop little bunnies, hop, hop, hop.
Hop little bunnies, hop, hop, hop.
Hop little bunnies - hop, hop, hop.
Stop little bunnies, stop, stop, stop!

22

Chapter Two

SUMMER

Beltane   Summer Solstice

As well as making our own songs and chants together, I also like to introduce some well known folk songs which I think enriches our celebrations. Traditional old rhymes and poems set to music, and some circle dancing is lovely whether in a ritual setting or elsewhere. I'm also keen on using natural resources and recycled bits and bobs for our craft activities wherever possible. This is a good lesson to teach young children that will hopefully stay with them whether Pagan or not.

Our summer time is a great one whether it's a traditional British summer (with the odd downpour), or a warmer one. When my eldest two children were growing up, I lived in Essex and arranged weekend camps to celebrate the festivals at a friend's farm through the summer months. Inviting other groups along with their families was great fun, often people volunteering an hour or two to give a workshop. We would make a communal veggie stew to cook on the fire pit while we had our celebrations. Afterwards we would all sit and share a meal round the fire, while the musicians amongst us played guitars, mandolins and drums. The children always enjoyed these camping experiences and it was wonderful to sleep out under the stars. You may find a local farmer happy to let you and your children to camp out for a night or two - you will still enjoy the experience even without the fire pit and big outdoor 'party'. Camping is always a great adventure for children. If you have an enclosed garden why not use that? It's another great way to get close to nature.

Beltane

The weather should be quite warm now, although our climate can often throw up some unexpected challenges! The blossoms will be fully out, the seeds planted in the gardens and the young animals will have been born. This is the beginning of summer. A fertility festival, it is the sacred marriage between the Goddess and the God where she becomes pregnant with life while the crops grow. It is a fire festival and fires were lit for people to jump to ensure fertility. Herds of cattle were led between two bonfires to do the same.

In earlier times this would be the time of the woodland weddings, where young couples would spend the night together in the forests, and if a child was conceived they might stay together as husband and wife. There were many May Day spells - such as washing your face in the dew on May Day to ensure beauty and to attract a husband. Often a May queen was chosen - a representation of the Goddess, and her consort the Green Man is still seen carved into old churches that stand on ancient Pagan sites.

There are lots of old traditions and customs still alive today at this time. The hobbyhorse - probably at one time a dragon figure, dances around some villages to bring life and energy to the crops. At Rochester in Kent, the Morris climb

Bluebell Hill to Kits Coty a local sacred site, at night to dance the may day dawn in. Then the sweeps festival takes place over 3 days. As always I like to look for events to mark the season and take the children to wherever possible. There are many other local festivals - you may even find a maypole to dance around.

As well as participating in local events, as usual we will begin preparations several days before with excursions into the countryside. We will pick some leaves off an Oak tree - remembering to ask and thank the tree. Looking for greenery to decorate the altar, we will particularly look for Hawthorn, which traditionally should only be brought into the house at Beltane to avoid bad luck. If you have flowers in bloom in your garden, you may want to cut some for the altar. I have usually potted some marigolds, which will go on the altar too.

We will make honey cakes to have on the altar, and a similar custom to stirring the Xmas cake means each person stirs the honey mixture making a wish before it is put into bun cases for baking. They can be iced with a little red and white flower on the top when cool if you want.

We will have a picnic as usual outdoors. If we find a tree with a fairly branchless lower trunk, we may turn it into a temporary maypole, with crepe paper red and white ribbons to dance round. It's a bit chaotic and the ribbons tear with the enthusiastic pulling, but the paper can be torn down afterwards and taken away so not to litter the area. You can also make a small indoor maypole to put bring out each year.

Before our walk we will have cut rice paper lip and heart shapes out to write a summer wish. We can stick these onto branches of trees knowing the paper will disintegrate and not affect the environment adversely. Occasionally the children eat them before they get as far as being stuck on a tree, but one way or another the earth is receiving the request!! We may also collect flowers from the gardens of friends (with their permission) to press for making pretty cards and summer pictures later.

Beltane has some similarities to Samhain insofar that it has a thin veil between the worlds. Hence the lord of misrule may be about and though we will not get the trick or treating of Halloween, fun games like tag, what's the time mister wolf and other gentle teasing is enjoyed on our walk. At home the children like to make tissue flowers - pink or red roses with green leaves and we can make them up in wreathes to hang over the altar or on the doors. We will also make Green Man masks out of paper plates with the Oak leaves gathered on our outing to the wood. For older children, you could make salt dough or hobby clay Green Men to paint and hang on the walls. Another thing for the children to make is a daisy chain either real or from paper. We make up little crowns of fresh flowers to crown the little girls as May Queens for our ceremony, and Green leaf ones for the boys to crown them as Jack i' the Green. And if you want to be a bit adventurous what about making a hobbyhorse for the children to play on.

The celebrations will begin with a procession into the circle area led by the children crowned as May Queens and Kings. However all the participants may wear flowers if they wish. The altar is decorated with the children's artwork and red and white flowers and ribbons.

The circle is cast and the Goddess invited in. We then toast the Lord of Misrule followed by a hearty rendition of *'Summer is i' coming in'*. We will write little wishes onto heart-shaped paper similar to the ones on our walk, but these will be burned by candle flame in a cast iron cauldron, heavily supervised!

The children will have a story - perhaps snow white and rose red, or beauty and the beast. Any family blessings or songs will be sung and particularly those in the round. We may make little poppets to bless our home and our personal harvests this year. Finally the cauldron with the candle will be placed in the centre and everyone will jump the flame. It may be that the children will need to be passed over it from one adult to another for safety. Older children will be able to manage it themselves as long as they lift their clothing high above the flame - use your common sense for this. Finally the honey cakes and grape juice is blessed and shared before closing the circle. Feasting takes place before the children retire to well earned sleep.

Making the Items for the Festival

Portable Maypole

Get a piece of doweling from the local DIY store cut to a length of about 2 - 3 metres. This will depend if you want to use it indoors as well as out, and the height of your ceilings! Drill a hole through the top about 2 centimetres from the top through the diameter and thread string through the hole tying the ends together. Cut equal numbers of red and white ribbon for twice the length of the pole and attach to the top, just under the drilled hole.

If you use it indoors, you will need to suspend it from a fixed beam or hook inserted into the ceiling and something to hold or weigh it down at the bottom. I have seen something similar to a xmas tree support made to hold it still from the bottom. If used outside, push it into the ground like a sun umbrella used at the beach. Another way is to do away with the pole altogether and just suspend ribbons from the hook in the ceiling.

Green Man Masks

Collect small paper plates, leaves gathered from trees you have pressed, or cut tissue paper leaves. Draw a face on the plate and cut out holes for eyes and mouth. Stick the leaves with PVC glue around the face fanning outward and insert some into the eye and mouth holes. Attach a ribbon or string to the top and hang to decorate. Or attach string on either side to wear.

Tissue flowers

Take pink and red tissue for roses, and white and yellow for daisies. Fold several layers in a concertina fold and secure in the centre with green pipe cleaners. Add green cut tissue leaves if you wish. Crinkle open the layers to represent petals. Arrange in hoop shapes to hang around the home or on the door as wreaths.

Poppets

These are little dolls you can make with material. Handkerchief size white cotton folded into a triangle. A ball of cotton wool or other stuffing is put in the centre of the fold and tied around with wool to create a head. A further tie of wool a little way down to create a waist will force the two points on either side to look like arms. Wool can be sewn or stuck on the head for hair and pens or stitches form eyes, nose and mouth. If you want to insert something in the padding such as a small crystal or anything written is up to you.

You can decorate with strips of material tied round like clothing. These are blessing poppets to represent the spirit of Beltane to hang in the home for abundance. It's best to have a red one and a white one and hang them in pairs.

Hobby Horse

Get a piece of doweling from a DIY shop cut about 1 metre long. With Papier-mache make a horse's head shape and insert it on the top of one end of the pole. Put it somewhere to dry for a few days.

When dried, paint it brown or black. Make a wool mane and stick it on the head. Add a ribbon stuck around the neck and across the nose like a bridle. If you prefer, you could cut out some black or brown felt in the shape of the head and fill it with stuffing or sand when you sew it up. Attach this to the pole and finish off with the mane and ribbon.

Songs

To the Greenwood (a round)

Come follow, follow, follow, follow, follow, follow me
Whither shall I follow, follow, follow?
Whither shall I follow, follow thee?
To the Greenwood, to the Greenwood, to the Greenwood,
Greenwood Tree.

Summer Solstice - Litha

The summer solstice is the longest day celebrating the height of the summer and the God of nature, before his powers wane as we travel once more towards the winter months. This was a time when people would gather on hilltops to light great bonfires and dance around them. Healers might gather their herbs to dry and store for medicines and wine recipes as the sun is strong and lends its energy to the plants. I have a mixture of herbs growing on my balcony, some for culinary use and some for magical use whether medicinal or for home made incenses. Children love to grow plants and its fun for them to grow sunflowers to harvest the seeds when the flowers begin to wilt. I will usually gather in some of the herbs to dry and grind to store for the rest of the year.

It is at this time the Oak King is celebrated as the Holly King takes his turn to rule. You could gather oak leaves on your country walks which would be potent with solar energy - they make a good dry white wine to keep for next year. On our outings leading up to the festival as we have a hilly area nearby, we take baby round cheeses on our walk and have fun rolling them and racing down the hill. We race them in their wrappers and if the wrapping is still intact we can eat the cheese afterwards. If you feel more adventurous you could get a larger round cheese and roll it too. I tell the children the cheese represents the sun and people used to roll really large cheeses. We make jokes that it's not the moon but the sun that should be made of cheese.

There are lots of midsummer fetes and flower festivals in the local villages around this time. We also like to go to the local seaside carnivals throughout the summer too, and collect more seashells for making pictures. You may want to look for one or two larger pebbles on the beach. We will take them home and paint pictures on them of flowers or suns -

making paperweights to give as gifts. Or we may paint animal totems on them.

We collect more flowers and leaves for pressing and make cards with flowers and sunbursts for our friends. We may wind fresh flowers around a circle to hang as a wreath in the home, or possibly make another tissue paper one of pink and white roses. We will cut out butterfly shapes and ladybirds and paint and decorate them to hang in the room too.

Before our circle, the children make tissue stained glass hangings to hang in the window. We might make salt dough or hobby clay sunbursts to paint and hang over the altar. We may also make bunting or streamers to hang on the balcony and on the windows - in the four quarter colours of yellow, red, blue and green.

Our picnic may be in the woods, by the sea or even the local park where we take balls and games and teddies for a teddy bears' picnic! We pack lots of strawberries too, and at home we make lots of scrumptious strawberry jam for the store cupboard or as gifts.

The room is decorated with all the things we've made and with as many yellow and orange flowers as we can get. I often ask guests to bring extra flowers with them so we can have our own flower festival! We have bowls of strawberries and cherries on the altar instead of cakes. As it's another light festival, I like to have lots of pretty candles lit - though up out of the reach of the children. With flowers and candles on the higher shelves, the area looks very pretty. We will open the circle in the usual way and invite the Goddess.

With children attending, I think it best that activities such as Drawing Down the Moon or the symbolic Great Rite with the Five-Fold Kiss are left out for adult-only circles as they can be quite powerful. I may have Full Moon meetings for my groups, which may involve intense meditation and energy work. These are not like our gentle family festival celebrations so more powerful work is left for the adult meetings. We do have a Five-Fold Blessing adapted for including the children, which I will describe at the end of this section.

We will have a story such as the competition between the Wind and the Sun. Or perhaps an adventure of Robin Hood. We also tell the children how we need the sun to ripen the corn, and to give us the food we need to live and to make vitamins for our health.

In the circle we will have small sun shapes cut out on yellow card to write wishes and blessings on which we will burn by candle flame in a small cast iron cauldron - supervised as usual. As at this time the Goddess is pregnant with the ripening grain we will have blessings and prayers asking for a good abundant harvest.

The Five-Fold Blessing is done with everyone and then two unlit candles are lit to represent the Midsummer Fires. Everyone passes between the two candles and is anointed on the forehead with sacred oil (usually orange and lemon oil well diluted with a carrier oil such as almond. We will have a dance next and we will probably have taken in bells and tambourines to get a Morris effect when we dance. After family and guests blessings we will bless the cherries and strawberries and share them. Finally the circle is closed and we share our feast before the children are off to bed.

Items to make for the festival

Tissue Stained glass window hangings

Take a paper plate and cut out the middle. Cut out strips and shapes of yellow, orange and red tissue paper and stick together. Attach this to the centre of the paper plate and hang from a ribbon or string in the window.

Alternatively, get a plastic plate or container lid. Stick the strips of tissue to the plate with PVC glue and coat over the top with a thin layer of glue. When it's dry, peel the tissue picture off the plate and fasten in the centre of the paper plate or stick onto the window for a stained glass effect.

Summer bunting

With either coloured tissue paper or scraps of material, cut out lots of long triangular flags then stick them to a long piece of strong string or cord. Hang around the room or from windows or balcony (I used to do a really long one and hang it from the two posts of a washing line in the garden - it always looked very festive!).

Sacred Solar Oil

Take some orange oil and lemon oil (about 10 drops of each) and mix with 50 drops or carrier oil such as sweet almond or oil seed rape. Tap bottle gently to mix for about 5 minutes then leave in the sun for a full day, after which put into a dark cupboard away from the light. During a Full Moon rite consecrate with all elements in your own traditional way.

Five Fold Blessing

This is nice to do in pairs but is fine as singular too.

Touch feet and say;		*'Blessed be my (thy) feet that walk on the Earth*
Touch knees	-	*'Blessed be my (thy) knees that kneel on the Earth*
Touch tummy	-	*'Blessed be my (thy) body that is nourished by the Earth*
Touch chest	-	*'Blessed be my (thy) heart that beats the rhythm of the Earth*
Touch lips	-	*'Blessed be my (thy) lips that speak with freedom on the Earth.*

Chapter Three

AUTUMN

Lughnasadh   Autumn Equinox

One of the really fun things is making the various tools and robes or dresses with the children for them to use in the circle. I've already talked about making a little wand to use, and you can really go to town and make a complete set of children's tools if you wish, although I personally think children are too young for an athame. If you make a white robe for your child, they can have fun tie-dyeing it whatever colours they choose. Or you can get fabric pens and let them go to town putting their own designs on it. They may prefer a coloured one, and older children can help to stitch it or add beading and sequins to personalise it.

My groups wear clothing of their choice - it may be a special robe or something symbolic - I personally do not work in a skyclad tradition. I have no problem with nudity with other adults but I firmly believe it is not a good thing with children in the circle. There are some terrible things concerning the abuse of children happening today and even though the situation may be completely innocent, any child mentioning naked ceremonies is going to attract attention - and rightly so. At the beach, in the garden or in the home; if your child loves to strip off and enjoy the freedom of nudity, you are probably encouraging them to be confident and well adjusted about their bodies. But there is a right time and place - and the family festival circle is not it.

Lughnasadh

This is the early autumn harvest. A festival of lights - Lugh was a Celtic God of light. It was also known as Lammas by the early christians - basically meaning Loaf-Mass, to celebrate the first grain harvests of the year. This was traditionally a time for games and tribal competition, horse racing and trials of strength. A celebration of the Corn King. An early harvest of vegetables, grain and fruit before the final harvesting in late autumn. A major fruit crop starting its harvest now is the apple and there will be apple festivals in some local areas. Between Canterbury and Faversham in Kent is a large apple farm centre specifically growing many varieties of apple that are no longer grown elsewhere. There is often a fair or open day around this time, and in 2005 the apple was highly celebrated at the Canterbury Festival. The apple is a sacred fruit of the Goddess and if you cut across the core you will find a pentagram shape inside. It is also the time of the grape harvest and although not known as a British fruit, it has actually been grown here since ancient times.

I like to look for fetes and other events as usual. Perhaps we may have a trip to a local farm shop or the farmers market to buy organic cider and apples. We have our country walks to collect some greenery for the altar and a picnic to take with us. Another outing could be to the local park to play games like rounders or scavenging games with a list of items to find or cross off when discovered. We may have some fun races - perhaps a relay race, three-legged or sack races if we have enough participants to join in. I will most likely arrange a picnic and invite other families to join us in the local park, but you may wish to do this in your own garden if you have one big enough. There are some seaside festivals to visit, folk music festivals and oyster festivals all near my home, and these are echoed up and down the country. I also like to have an outing out to the countryside just to look at the expanses of wheat and cornfields before the combine-harvesters cut them down. There is something very beautiful and tranquil about fields of grain waiting to be harvested and it never fails to move me.

We will also make bread - although I have a bread machine, this bread really needs to be made completely by hand, kneaded and prepared personally. Children often enjoy making bread and seeing the 'magic' as it doubles in size after leaving it to rise. We will have fun making different shapes - cottage loaves, rolls and plaits. This bread will be to share and to leave outside as offerings, but we can also make salt dough bread plaits to paint and thread with ribbons to hang as decoration.

Once again your family may like to make cards to give to your Pagan friends, and we also like to make lanterns to hang outdoors if possible. Nowadays you can buy strings of lights to hang in the home - like the xmas tree lights but often with different shapes and designs. Outdoor lanterns or even outdoor oil lamps or candles on bamboo that is speared into the soil. The children can make simple Chinese lanterns of folded paper for decoration but obviously cannot be put near a candle flame. As it is also a harvest of the sea we may have made decorative items with seashells and sea pictures. We can take oyster shells and make a necklace of them - or paint them with runes or other symbols. You may like to make seashell-decorated gifts like photo frames or knick-knack boxes with shells on top.

Our celebrations begin in the usual way. The altar is decorated with greenery, seashells and candlelight. There are bowls of apples and grapes, and the loaves of plaited bread. Around the room are the decorations made by the children.

After the circle is opened and the Goddess invited in, we also invite and welcome the Corn King. There will be a story for the children - perhaps the tortoise and the hare. We will sing some songs such as the chant 'we all come from the Goddess' accompanied with drumming, followed by a spiral dance to the accompaniment of singing of Robert Burns' *Once upon a Lammas Night*. Some apples will be cut in half and a small piece of paper with a wish written on it will be sandwiched between the two halves which is then tied together. This will be buried in a garden and as it decomposes, the energy of the wish is released. Any family or guest's blessings and prayers will be made, followed by the blessing of the bread and juice which is shared. The circle is closed and as usual we feast together before the children retire to bed.

Items to make for the festival

Chinese Lanterns

Take 2 pieces of A4 coloured paper or decorate and painted and stick them together in as a long piece. Alternatively, cut paper to size. Fold it in half longways and cut equal slits across the fold leaving a border uncut on both edges. Unfold the paper and join the two shorter edges together in a tube shape - squashing it out slightly to reveal slats that would allow light through if used as a lampshade. Attach ribbon or string to one end to hang.

Soda Bread

This is a very easy bread to make without yeast and takes less than 30 minutes including cooking time. Enough self raising flour, some oil seed rape or sunflower oil and milk with 1 teaspoon bicarb - adding the milk slowly and knead until you get a doughy consistancy. You can add spices or herbs if you wish. Cinnamon and sultanas are lovely, or some large chunks of cheese embedded in the dough. Bake at about 200c or gas 5 for 20 minutes or so, until its golden on top and sounds hollowish if knocked. (mind though - its hot!) You can have this with butter, dunked in soup and pass it round for the cakes and ale.

Songs

We All Come From the Goddess (can be sung in the round)

We all come from the Goddess, and to her we shall return
Like a drop of rain falling to the ocean
Hoof and horn, hoof and horn
All who die shall be reborn.
Corn and grain, corn and grain
All who fall shall rise again (repeat all as required)

Autumn Equinox - Modron

This is another time of balance with the day and night being equal in length before the slide down into shorter days and the cold dark nights of winter. The end of the harvests when all must be safely gathered in to store for the introspective time of winter and life sleeps under the earth. This is a time of thanksgiving. We thank the Earth for her bounties and what she has given us and contemplate the darkness ahead. The hard work of the harvests has come to an end and we can rest and celebrate awhile before the storing and drying or bottling and preservation of the fruit and grain must be done. The early harvest of Lughnasadh is a time where the sacrifice of the Corn God is celebrated. The end of the harvests at the equinox is a celebration of the abundance of the Earth.

I always feel the changes of the seasons more keenly at the equinox's whether spring or autumn. I think this is because, although a balance, it is a time when people slip into a 'different gear'. Our bodies are winding down for the winter, our minds psychologically preparing for longer nights and more time out of the elements. In the spring we are 'waking up' and preparing to get out in the sun.

We will try to have lots of walks and outings over this time, being aware that the weather during the winter months may not allow too many excursions with young children. We will look for harvest type events in the local paper. Although unlikely to attend a christian harvest festival, we may visit some of the older churches nearby to search for signs of the green man or other Pagan symbols. My children are being taught to celebrate Pagan festivals but I still want them to appreciate and understand other beliefs and respect them too. Our walks to the woods will produce some greenery to decorate the altar. We especially look for hedgerows with an abundance of blackberries which we pick and put into pies, cakes or even the demi-john!

Another trip to any nearby cornfields that have been harvested will be undertaken to see if we can find a few pieces left behind that we can take home to make corn dollies. Or you can knock on the farmer's door and ask permission to cut a few stalks before the harvest has been finished. There are lots of books that give instructions on making corn dollies from simple weaves to extremely complicated ones. We will make simple corn dollies to hang up over the altar. One new corn dolly will be hung up after the ritual to await his new bride at next years Imbolg celebration.

We make cards to give to our friends with corn and harvest pictures on them, and we write a list which may take several days to think of, of all the abundance we have received in the last year that we can be grateful for. There are other seaside harvests to appreciate and although fishing is a yearlong activity, this was the time when it became harder and less frequent with bad weather in more ancient times. So we include the harvest of the sea in our celebrations too. We may pick up some strands of seaweed to put on the altar (it can go in the garden with compost afterwards if you wish), and if available collect samphire.

We will have another bread making session again, this time making a loaf in the shape of a corn dolly with a face. This is John Barleycorn the spirit of the Fields. We will also make preserves and jams for the winter and bottle fruit. If you have an allotment or garden veggie patch this is a great time to celebrate harvesting your produce and you may want to hang some of your decorations around the site as you finish lifting your vegetables and fruit. I also like to make lemon and honey syrup or cinnamon candies for colds and sore throats that may occur during the winter. Children always seem to love helping with these activities and eating or drinking things they have helped to make. Again it also helps them make a connection between themselves and the Earth that feeds them.

I will have asked any guests to visit earlier with a bag of vegetables and fruit. Most of it will go on the altar as decoration of the harvests. I will make up a vegetable soup or stew with the rest, and perhaps stew the fruit or make a pie. This is to warm up and share after the circle is closed.

The celebration begins with the circle opening as usual followed by the invitation to the Goddess. The altar has been decorated with greenery, corn, bread, fruit and nuts. Any one who feels they have a personal harvest they wish to celebrate may have an object to symbolise it placed on the altar. We will follow the circle opening with some songs or rhymes for the children to join in, such as *'Oats and Beans and Barley grows'* while we have a spiral dance. We will also have a story for the children - perhaps 'the very hungry caterpillar' for the younger ones.

Last year's corn dolly and Brighid doll are also on the altar - symbolising the Earth Mother and Corn King and we thank them for the last year's abundance. Afterwards they will be buried or burned in a garden bonfire with a simple blessing. Our lists of personal harvests will be read out with prayers of gratitude for what we have achieved this last year and any guest who has a token on the altar may talk about what it means.

We will bless the John Barleycorn loaf and bread on the altar with the grape juice and some of it will be shared. Then we close the circle. Afterwards the stew is warmed up and served with the rest of the bread followed by the pie. The rest of the vegetables and fruit is bagged up and next day its taken to a local old peoples' home or hospice as a gift from a 'folklore society' harvest festival!!

Items to make for the Festival

Corn Dollies

Take several long stalks of corn and soak overnight to soften. Tie together under the sheaf head then plait the stalks evenly as required. Bend in a circle and fasten as a loop. Decorate with red ribbon.

Alternatively - leave un-soaked and separate into 2 separate bundles. Tie one bundle under the sheaf head - this is the body. Then separate the other bundle into 2 again and tie both under the sheaf heads. Insert the thinner bundles on either side to form arms on the body like an equal arm cross so that the sheaf heads on them form the hands. Secure and tie with red ribbon. Separate the body under the tie into 2 legs and tie with ribbon.

(Though not for the festival I thought you might like the recipes I use for the winter sore throat soothers).

Honey and lemon syrup

Squeeze 10 lemons and add to 6 oz honey and 2 oz glycerine. Mix by shaking thoroughly and put into sterilised bottle. Keep out of the light. It should last all winter. I use Manuka honey for its anti-biotic properties but any runny honey is fine.

Cinnamon Candies

Take equal weights of cinnamon and sugar. Mix together. Take a couple of ounces of gum arabic and mix with lemon juice to make a thick syrup and mix with the cinnamon mix until like a very thick paste. Roll out and cut into small circular sweets of about 2cms. Leave to dry for a few days and store in a dry jar.

48

Chapter Four

WINTER

Samhain   Winter Solstice

This is a terrific time to really enjoy getting to know the phases of the Moon and looking at the stars. The earlier darkening sky means little ones are still likely to be up when the sun goes down and some serious sky watching can occur. Although I don't have them participating in my Coven Esbats or circles timed for the phases of the Moon, I still think that my children can learn what their effects are and what they symbolise. As our bodies are over 90% water and the Moon effects the ebb and flow of the tides, it seems sensible to note the different phases in the same way that we acknowledge the cycle of the seasons and its effects on us.

Our group's Moon phase circles are likely to be more powerful and we are usually doing some kind of magical work. Most Wiccans believe that as children are still developing emotionally, mentally and spiritually till their late teens, the participation in more powerful rites may be detrimental to them.

There is one occasion I make an allowance and that is when a young girl has her first menstrual period. Then a full moon ritual will be arranged with women only in attendance to celebrate her and make a fuss of her becoming a woman.

You may have seen weather clocks made for young children's television programmes with the hours of the clock replaced with sunny, cloudy, windy, snowy and rainy weather. You might like to make a Moon Phase clock with Full, Waning, Dark/New and Waxing Moon symbols on it, which the children can keep an eye on the Moon's changing cycles. It's easy to make and you can let the children decorate it and choose a place to keep it - it is their tool really after all.

It's also nice to get an astronomy star chart and put it on a child's bedroom wall. On clear nights you can plot the stars together, or have competitions to find various constellations. This is the time for cosy stories too and the myths and stories of how the stars got their names.

You may like to take the children on Moon light walks. This is something that the Woodcraft Folk suggest in their organiser's handbook, and I can't recommend it highly enough. It gives the children a different perspective on things they usually only see in daylight. It's a magical 'between the worlds' type of feeling. Take them to a park to go on the swings in the early evening when it's dark, looking up to see if you can spot bats flying above.

Some nature reserves and forestry commission woodlands have special organised walks to spot night wildlife at this time of year. It is a sad thing but important to note that if you do go out for night walks yourself, it is best to go with other adults too - there's safety in numbers, and of course it is very important to impress on children not to go out alone in the dark.

Samhain

I love all the different festivals in the year but I do have a sneaky extra fondness for Samhain. This is a very magical time - like Beltane it's a time when the veil between the worlds is very thin. The Lord of Misrule is about and mischief abounds. I've often heard people complaining that the 'trick or treat' custom is an American import but it echoes the memories from earlier folk customs that the faery walk abroad at this time of year - the Piskies of Cornwall, the leprechauns of Ireland. Children love this aspect of Samhain and the stories of mischievous sprites.

We can really get into the spirit of it fairly early on. The shops these days are full of masks and costumes, fake cobwebs, cakes and pumpkins a few weeks before - as Halloween is celebrated all over the country. If the weather is agreeable we will visit the woods to pick up some greenery to decorate the altar. We will also look for early chestnuts and sloes. We may make cards to send to our friends with bats, owls and friendly ghosts on them. A visit to the local farm shop or farmers' market to pick up a couple of pumpkins is a must. One to serve pumpkin soup in, and another to carve and stand a candle in for the spirit of Samhain.

We can make paper-plate pumpkins to hang around the room to decorate. We will also hang paper skeletons around, cut bats out of black paper and hang them up. A few years ago I acquired a hairdressers dummy head which we hung up with painted blood! The point is that the scary element of Samhain is important. It teaches children to laugh at fears which takes the power of fear away. It also introduces them to the concept of death and decay, which happens to everyone. These days death is rarely encountered in everyday life, our dead are 'spirited away' by funeral directors whereas once upon a time we would lay out our dead, pay our respects with the wake, sit with them and administer to them up to the burial. People become scared of something they don't have to face head on that often. In Mexico there is a festival of the dead and other cultures will have a meal at the graveside of their ancestors.

When I ran my first group we had a Samhain celebration that had lots of games and a symbolic journey to the underworld. It was so much fun that I adapted it to enable it to be used in a family situation. We decorate the room with the paraphernalia described earlier. The altar is decorated with the greenery from the woods, the pumpkin with its lit candle and apples. Over the door to the room is hung a wispy curtain of ragged silk or chiffon. In the kitchen a washing up bowl contains apples floating in water with plenty of towels available! Everyone is asked to make a list of friends, family, ancestors and pets that are no longer living and they wish to remember and honour. They also bring lots of party food for the Feast of the dead.

We begin by opening the circle and inviting the Goddess. We may have some fun scary stories with actions like 'we're all going on a bear hunt'. We might all chant the witches' rune - 'Darksome night and shining Moon'. We will sit together and make 'eyes of light' which will be hung in the home during winter to draw light to the hearth. The chalice of fruit juice will be blessed. After this everyone except one person will be blindfolded. That person will cut a doorway in the circle and lead each person one by one through the 'veil' into the kitchen - the reason for this will become clear later. We take the chalice of juice with us. Younger children don't usually like things over their eyes so we'll just bring them through without. Once in the kitchen, which represents the under-world, we will each read out our lists of family etc that we want to honour. The chalice is then passed around to toast those we remember.

This may be a good time to talk about what happens when we die. Whether you believe the soul returns to the elements and nature, or in re-incarnation, or you have other ideas - its something you could want to discuss with your children. You may prefer to do so privately - some children may have lots of questions and some may not be ready to talk about it or discuss in front of friends.

Having taken a trip to the kitchen 'underworld', in order to come back to the living world we must undertake the ordeal of water. The ordeal of water is apple bobbing!! Hence the kitchen representing the underworld and the towels available. If you have a sheltered patio or yard, you could do this bit outside as it can get a bit messy! Make sure you have dry clothing available for the children afterwards though. The party food can be taken from the kitchen back into the circle. The centre piece is a pumpkin shell filled with warm pumpkin broth. Once back in the circle the cut doorway can be closed any family or guest's blessings can be given. The feasting takes place in the circle before it is closed and a plate and wine glass are set with food and juice for the unseen guests remembered in the lists read out earlier. Finally the circle is closed and by this time the children will be ready for a good night's sleep.

Things to make for the Festival

Pumpkin Soup

Cut the top off the pumpkin and scoop the seeds out first. Then scoop the flesh out making sure you leave a good thick layer of skin and flesh to become a soup 'pot'. Boil up the thinly cut flesh with an onion, garlic, pepper and spices.

Add a couple of stock cubes and simmer for about 20 minutes. Cool and mix with half a pint of single cream, salt and pepper to taste. Blend it smooth and put in fridge. Heat it through and serve in the pumpkin skin with crusty bread.

Eye of Light

Take 2 thin branches of a tree or two thin sticks of about 30 cms length. Tie together in the shape of an equal armed cross. Take coloured ribbon or wool and wind around each arm of the cross from the centre outwards, weaving until you have made a web shape. Use different colours if you wish, joining them together by knotting. Hang in the home until Imbolg.

Winter Solstice - Yule

Another festival of light, the solstice is the shortest day and longest night before the Sun begins to warm the Earth and new growth begins. The rebirth of the Sun God. This is why christians have chosen this time to represent the birth of their son of God. It was a chink of light in dark, cold times to encourage the people to hold on until the Spring. Most of December is celebrated in our society as the advent before xmas.

There are lots of things going on, you can take the children to see Father Xmas, there are pantomimes to visit and you can tell the children how they originated from mummers plays and folk stories. We go to xmas fayres and watch parades or winter carnivals if there are any. In Canterbury there is the parade of Saint Nicholas that ends up at the Cathedral with lots of school children processing through the City streets. I always enjoy carol singing regardless of their mostly christian connection. There are lots of wassail songs and more Pagan ones like the Holly and the Ivy to enjoy too. It's good fun to go out carolling and collect for charity if you can.

I put a xmas tree up at the beginning of December with cinnamon sticks and pine cones which children can paint and decorate with glitter. If you put the cinnamon behind the xmas lights, the warmth of the bulb spreads a lovely cinnamon smell into the room. We make clove oranges, lemons and limes and put in a bowl to scent the room too. Or you can dry slices of orange and lemon and hang on the tree. We do at least one country walk to collect any greenery for the altar. Ivy and Holly are wonderful but remember that Ivy is poisonous. So too is mistletoe, so make sure if you have young children that they cannot get hold of the berries.

We make traditional paper chains and streamers to hang around the room. Fold up white paper to make pretty snow flakes to stick on the windows and snowmen with brightly coloured hats and scarves. We also make Yule cards to send to friends and family, and try to make as many of our presents as possible. We collect pretty jars and ketchup bottles during the year, which I will clean and sterilise for us to fill with olive oil and herbs from the balcony. We can make pepper-mint and orange oil creams and fudge or truffles. Another thing which children love to help you make is a gingerbread house to set in the centre of your ritual feast. Or gingerbread biscuits to hang on the tree or give as gifts.

Although we have juice for the chalice, I do like to make a mulled wine or cider to warm up the adult guests when they first arrive. The festival celebrations begin with opening the circle. The altar is decorated with any greenery. There are nuts, apples, oranges and figs surrounding a decorated unlit candle. A chocolate Yule log and chalice of juice to one side, and a bowl of the clove fruit with ribbons attached to give to all our ritual guests.

The Goddess is invited in and we light the Yule candle in the centre of the altar as I don't have a fireplace for a Yule log. If you do have a fireplace then its wonderful to have a proper Yule log for the occasion. The children will have a story - possibly the night before xmas or little robin red vest. We will sing the Holly and the Ivy and Here we come a Wassailing while we have a spiral dance. Everyone is given a small taper candle to light from the centre Yule candle to light our way through the winter.

Obviously the children are supervised holding the candles. We will all stand holding the lit candles and family and guest blessings for the seasons will be made. Then the candles are put out for safety and the chalice and chocolate Yule log are blessed and shared. One of the children will take the bowl of clove fruit around and give one to everyone with a wish of 'light and warmth for the winter'.

Finally the circle is closed and we all sit to feast while any seasonal gifts are exchanged. Then its goodnight to the children as they go off to bed. Of course with non-Pagan family members celebrating xmas, we will also have xmas day and xmas presents on the 25th December like the rest of the country, so all in all, we do very nicely with the season of goodwill!

Things to make for the Festival

Clove Fruit

Take clean washed unblemished oranges, lemons and limes and jars or cloves.

Use a fork to press small holes into the fruit in patterns all over. Put a clove in each of the holes. When complete, tie pretty coloured ribbon around each piece of fruit and secure with a pin. Hang in a warm airing cupboard or dry overnight in a slightly warm oven. I have had fruit that have lasted and retained the scent for several years. In a bowl by a radiator they smell heavenly.

Orange, lemon and lime slices to hang on the tree, or wind into a wreath

Slice the fruit into thin slices. Gently squeeze the juice out into a bowl (you can drink this or use in cooking. Wrap the slices in a towel and stomp on it to get more juice out. (We have great fun doing the stomping dance!) You can either put the over a warm radiator, an aga if you have one, or in the oven on a very low heat for a couple of hours. leave them on a plate in a warm room for a few days and you have nicely dried sliced fruit to decorate.

Gingerbread stained window biscuits

Using any gingerbread recipe, roll out dough and cut into arched window shapes. Cut holes out of the centre and place a coloured boiled sweet in the hole. Make a hole in the top to fit a ribbon through later. Bake the gingerbread according to recipe instructions. You will find the boiled sweet melts and makes the coloured glass effect of stained windows. When cool, tie ribbons through top hole and hang on xmas tree.

Sweets

Make peppermint or orange creams with icing sugar and water, and either peppermint or orange oil - just a few drops will be enough. Add colouring if required - green for peppermint, or orange colour. Roll the sugar dough into balls or flat and cut into shapes. Melt some good quality dark chocolate and dip half the sweets into chocolate, put to dry on greaseproof paper. Put into little sweet cases and wrap in cellophane with gold ribbon to tie.

Mulled Wine or Cider

Take a bottle of good red wine or cider. Add a sliced orange, apple and lemon, 4oz sugar, cinnamon sticks and cloves. A pinch of nutmeg and ginger. Warm on a slow flame but do not boil. Leave to gently simmer for about 5 minutes. Strain and serve with slices of the fruit floating in it

Chapter Five

Thoughts on Pagan Parenting

Archetypes   Outside Influences

Archetypes

I wrote in previous chapters regarding my feelings on working with the Moon phases. I will repeat that I do not include children in the Moon circle celebrations. I also run a group and am teaching students of The Craft and I think they might find it a bit of a hindrance having children included in the circle all the time. As I mentioned before, these times are really for our deeper magical aspects and spiritual develop-ment - and children need to develop as people first. That is not to say they are not spiritual beings, far from it.

However I do encourage them to learn about the changes of the Moon cycles and to acknowledge them - perhaps using the Moon Phase Clock we made together. We talk about the meanings of each different quarter and how it can affect us. The older ones can also find it helpful to understand how we are all affected by these cycles, if a friend is being a bit crabby, they might make allowances knowing what other influences there are in our lives.

Other major effects on the individual personality of course are the planetary influences and I think a little understanding of astrology when they're old enough is also a good thing. When my son was about 8 years old, his schoolteacher who knew I was a Pagan and interested in 'alternative' things asked me to come into his class and give a talk on astrology. This was quite a challenge, to try and explain to young children in a way they would find interesting and be able to understand without talking down to them, yet not swamp them with too much. I have kept the notes since then because I find them helpful to use for this age group. I have included the information in Appendix 2 and hope you will find it useful.

On our walks I have made a point of talking about the elements and what they are. I have not included them in our family book as correspondences as at some stage, if my children continue their wiccan lifestyles as young adults, they will probably start their own book of shadows. What I do think is that if they are interested and want to know, there are fun ways to learn about them. Obviously different weather can be utilised to point out the properties of earth, air, fire and water, and the different seasons will also be a good place to start. They may like to make their own charts or pictures if their interest is kindled. Home experiments with water and heat or learning to grow crystals are easy to research and you can probably find science kits and other interesting things in specialist shops if you wish. Or look in the library for book on children's fun science experiments. These are all good tools to learn about the physical effects of the elements and you can explain the mental and emotional ones too.

Learning about the Goddess and God, depends a lot on whether you follow a particular Wiccan tradition or pantheon. It may be natural for your seasonal celebrations to mention Isis or Cerridwen for instance, and I'm sure you will want to explain who they are and the stories about them to enrich your path together. As a traditional wiccan, I don't follow one particular tradition and so I teach my children all Goddess' are one Goddess, all Gods are one God. I can then illustrate things I want to teach by using different myths and stories. It may be a Greek story about Perseus or I may use one about Merlin or Isis. The point for me is that I have a wealth of information to fire their imaginations and understanding. And it widens their exposure to other cultures and lives. I will also use stories from the bible, Hinduism or eastern traditions if they illustrate my point, as they too are myths that have value. I want my children to be open individuals and respect other cultures and beliefs even if it's not their own.

When we have our seasonal celebrations we always invite the Goddess to be part of the circle. I have explained that the Goddess is always there, but we are acknowledging this and thanking her for always being available by doing this. Sometimes we might have a statue to represent her on our altar, or more often than not, we will have something from nature. I tend to refer to her as Mother Nature most of the time in conversation, although in the circle, she is the Lady or our Mother Goddess. I also talk about the God - mainly when the festival is particularly connected to Him. Again, he may be referred to as the Lord or any particular title of the season such as the Corn King.

I know that some Wiccans (usually Dianic tradition) prefer only to address the Goddess, while others are very particular about a balance of male and female energies. I personally have great affection and reverence for the God, but having been taught that the Goddess is first amongst equals, find I favour Her more. I tell you this because this book is describing my way of doing things and suggesting ideas, not instructing you how to be a Wiccan.

To learn about the different myths and stories of the Gods, I will use books, feature films, and anything else that can make it interesting as well as informative. If the children are old enough and show interest, you could do a research project together, drawing or painting pictures, going to archaeological or sacred sites together, there are so many things you can enjoy. There are some lovely books available for children now on the various stories and myths of the Gods - some of which are listed in Appendix 1.

Outside Influences

Education

This is a good time to mention a major outside influence you will encounter with children - School and education. Although Paganism is better accepted now than perhaps 10 years ago, you may still be unhappy with the rather un-spiritual way they are educated, and the social influences that they are exposed to there. There are two main things you can do;

> 1. Your child can attend the local school, where you can either keep your spiritual beliefs and activities private, or be completely open and make sure the teachers are well aware of your beliefs. I know this will depend on the school and you may have to wait for a while to judge the situation as to how open you can be. There is the argument that although we have our Pagan way of life, we still have to live in the world, and our children will have learned to integrate.

> 2. Or you can home-school which will give you a different situation and other possible difficulties. Our law at present states that we must make sure our

children receive an adequate education for their age in school or otherwise. It is the 'or otherwise' which allows us to teach them ourselves as long as that is what we are doing. Let's briefly look at both types of education with what I consider to be strengths and failures on either side.

Home Education

You are teaching your child from the moment she is born and its not only happening from nine in the morning to three in the afternoon, Monday to Friday. Your child is eager to learn, really wants to learn and is a sponge waiting for all that knowledge they desire. This means that you do not have to be a trained teacher to teach your children, nor does it have to follow a specific timetable.

At home there is no enforced curriculum or timing of sessions. If the child is interested in learning about the Romans and in school that subject is not done till next year's curriculum, they will have lost the momentum of their interest. The desire is here, now! You can explore together, visit sites, and do whatever you want to learn about the Romans. If they want to do nothing else for the next 3 weeks but Romans, that's ok. There's no 'having to stop painting Julius Caesar's flag because its time to do maths'.

If a child isn't ready to sit still for 20 minutes or more, they're not identified as difficult or fidgety. If they aren't ready to learn to read at 5 years old, they may be ready at 6 years and will do so with very few difficulties - because the desire is there. And of course, the child will get either individual attention, or share it with just a few others. You also teach them your own belief system and not the R.E curriculum someone else has set down. They are less influenced by the local trends or fashions and certainly wont be 'judged' in the playground for having the 'wrong' clothes or toys.

The downsides are the possibility of isolation - for you and the child. You really need to search out support groups and other home schooling parents. There are support organisations such as 'Education Otherwise' (see Appendix 1) and if there isn't a local one, perhaps you could start one up. Children need socialisation. However, I don't think that 30 children of the same age in one class is socialisation, a child needs to learn to relate to adults and children of different ages.

An effort is necessary on your part to make sure she has ample opportunity to mix with people regularly. Therefore, sport activities, dancing, music clubs, youth clubs etc are a must. Although I personally favour the idea of home education, I tend to try to be flexible, as it may be my child will thrive better in a more structured environment. You can only decide as you go along, and it may be the first few years are best at home, followed by a school education.

You may also find that their school-attending friends regard them as a bit of an oddity. Is that going to attract bullying? Is your child getting the opportunity to learn to cope away from you? So many important things that must be addressed.

For you personally, this means several years of being at home whether you want or need to earn a living or not. Is this something you can cope with? There are several books that discuss home education, which I have listed in Appendix 1.

I am fortunate that we do have support groups locally where I live for home educators. I have also joined with other parents to organise a local group of the Woodcraft Folk.

This is a fun club for children of all ages to get involved in games, crafts and camps with co-operative, nature based themes. I suppose you could say it's similar to the scouting movement, but although there is no religious bias or christian overtones, it is very Pagan friendly!! The head office address is in Appendix 1.

Another thing you could do is to start a weekly Pagan parenting group or coffee morning. It could be held in your home, or take it in turns to host it. Or you could arrange to meet at a local café. It's a good idea to sound out the idea with the Manager of the establishment, although I cant see them turning down regular custom! Its not really a place for having someone give a talk or discussion on Pagan subjects, more of a chance to meet up with like-minded parents and make a few friends as well as giving your children more chance to make friends too. I started a Pagan parents' lunch club'. Everyone brings some food, possibly a dessert or some lovely savoury bread, and I usually make a thick broth or spicy stew. We talk magic, children and anything else that takes our fancy, and the children chase each other and play and have a great time.

School Education

As I mentioned in the section about Home Education, your child may be one that needs the discipline and structure of the school system. And this is not a bad thing, some children thrive in this environment. It is your job as a parent to try and identify what they need and if you are able to, to give it to them. Your child may be the one that needs to be with a noisy class of 30 similar age children, it could be the ideal place to stimulate their desire to learn.

When teaching at home, you don't really turn off the lessons, the child may need to have a structure of a weekly learning session with weekends to let off steam. Of course parents of some faiths will use that time for other teaching - perhaps there will be religious classes or clubs they have to attend. The child may request to attend school. They may have friends that go there and want to be part of that, not wanting to feel left out or even lonely or alienated. Its very important that the child's feelings be taken into consideration. You may need to allow them to go to school to experience it if only to find out if they prefer one way or another.

You may need to work. There may be financial reasons that stop you from being able to stay at home. Or it may be that you cannot bear to be at home all the time. Some parents feel dreadfully guilty because they need to work for their own psychological health, believing they must be bad parents for not wanting to be with their children all the time. It must always be an individual decision taking the child's needs and the family needs as most important. The child's best interest is not being served if you stay at home feeling resentful because you need time away from her.

My older children were educated in school while I went out to work and afforded what might be considered a good standard of living. This time around, I live a far more simple life and hope to home educate depending on Rhiannon's needs. Which is best? It depends on the children - and you.

We live in a society that values money and consumables and is seemingly trying to institutionalise our young more and more, and as Pagans we may not like this, but we cannot fail to be influenced by it, even if it's not apparent. I have been in a situation as a working parent, and as parent on government benefits and it is easy to feel defensive or get caught up in assuming attitudes of superiority or feelings of 'guilt' - of believing that I must behave or believe in what society values. I can limit the damage by choosing not to watch TV or read newspapers, to go 'against' fashions and trends to try and express myself individually, but at the end of the day, I'm not going to be too hard on myself. You must do your best with what you can, and I don't believe there is any better way of parenting than that.

Chapter Six

Cause to Celebrate

Birth   Coming of Age   Requiem

Birth

This is not going to be a section on wiccaning. I don't believe in christening children - they are not able to make a choice as a baby whether to be dedicated to that religion, so I'm not going to be able to accept wiccaning for that same reason. However, I can and do celebrate the birth of children, and am more than happy to have a naming ceremony for my child. The child can be presented to the elements and blessings and gifts requested for them. Although I still will teach my children the Pagan way of living that I follow and hope to influence them, they will have the ultimate choice as adults whether to continue or reject my ideals.

My daughter Rhiannon was born at the beginning of February and so at the beginning of May, just after Beltane she was 3 months old. I felt this was a lovely time to hold a naming ceremony with the beginning of summer and it was held in a friend's garden. It was a small celebration with mainly friends and my older children attending. Grandparents were invited but being practising christians declined.

I had asked four of my closest friends to be 'Fairy God-mothers' and to think of a blessing or gift that they would like to wish upon my daughter. They had some wonderful qualities and blessings to 'give' her including the blessing of friendship - always to have good friends, and always to be a good friend to others, and beauty - to be able to see and appreciate beauty in all things and everyone. It was lovely to see how thoughtful they were in their blessings. Each one also gave her something to represent the gifts. One of the blessings was an appreciation and love of nature and my friend had planted 4 small trees in pots representing each season to be taken out and later planted in the wild.

It was a fairly simple celebration. My eldest children took Rhiannon to each quarter and we called the elements and presented her to each of them - symbolically naming her for their recognition. Each element was represented with an object - a feather for air, a candle for fire, a chalice for water and a crystal for earth. These were wrapped up after and put in a box for her to have, with photos and a copy of the ceremony for when she is older. I asked for a blessing on her from the Goddess and God and she was anointed with salt water and sacred oil. Finally we shared a chalice of wine and cake, followed by a lovely party with food and games for my friends' children. You can make up your own naming or birth celebration easily or do something similar to Rhiannon's day.

Birthdays

I don't tend to have a 'Pagan' celebration for a birthday, but I do like to acknowledge special ones and still may have a Pagan theme for them. When I celebrated my 40th birthday a few years ago, again, I asked a few friends to a meal I prepared to celebrate. For a week or so beforehand, I thought carefully and wrote a list of all the things I felt I had achieved or had meant something to me for each of the four decades I had lived so far. I shared this with my friends on my birthday, thanking the Goddess and God for all the abundance I had received thus far. I then claimed my next 40 years!! Followed with a good wine and a curry, it was a very satisfying and enjoyable birthday.

If you have a specific birthday milestone, or are arranging one for someone else, there are all kinds of variations on a theme to do this. You could ask family and friends to list qualities or achievements like I did for mine, or for a younger birthday such as 16 or 18, you could ask for blessings - similar to the naming ceremony for Rhiannon. Even nicer, (if not mortally embarrassing for a teenager) is to do it as a surprise.

Coming of Age

This is easier for girls rather than boys, for girls have a natural time for celebration of 'coming of age' which is when they begin the change into womanhood with the onset of their periods. Boys don't have a particular situation, you wouldn't really celebrate their voices changing and there isn't a marked move from boyhood to manhood. I would probably suggest that the 16th birthday for a boy is the best idea. It is a time when the child is legally able to leave school, which is a kind of initiation into the possible world of employment. It is an awkward age for a boy though, and their idea of birthday celebration may be something off with their friends rather than a Pagan gathering. I would have to play this one by ear.

A girl is easier in this case. When her body begins to change, breasts begin to bud and hair grows in more private areas, you will know her first period will not be far behind. I truly believe a lot of menstrual problems that women have suffered have been a result of negativity connected to menstruation, either from their families or society in general. Lets face it, it is called 'the curse' and the bible teaches Eve was 'afflicted' with it after tempting Adam with the apple. Tampons are still advertised on TV by slim young things, doing cartwheels on the beach with white trousers on. It is seen as something to get over with quickly and not mentioned in 'polite' conversation.

In more tribal societies, women who lived together usually bled together. It was seen as magical - a woman bled and didn't die. She was in her time of power and the men of the village would keep a distance - she was taboo, not because of inferiority, but because she was potent. How wonderful to teach our daughters that this is a time of power, of potency. Where we can be at our most creative. Where its ok to retreat from the world, to be introspective, thoughtful and to rest the body. Our society is one that says, be active, do, do, do! It is difficult if you are working or at school or college, to be reclusive for a few days, so we need to treat ourselves with kindness. Take relaxing baths. Go to bed early and read. Or sleep, in-between having to be up and at it in the world.

You can prepare her for her change beforehand, encouraging her to see it as positive and a cause to celebrate. Apart from the practicalities of how she is going to deal with it, whether to use pads, washable towels or a moon-cup. You can make an outing with her, visiting the chemists to look at what girls use. It's a private time for mothers and daughters. Buy or make a pretty box to keep her supplies in and place it somewhere she can see it, not hide it as though its something to be ashamed of.

When the magical day arrives, you can support her through her first time. Be gentle and sensitive to her fears and concerns. But be positive. For a girl's menstrual celebration, (and bear in mind she may not want to have a 'party') you can invite her closest girl friends and some of your women friends she knows and trusts. This is the one time I make an exception for a child to take place in a celebration of the Full Moon phase. This child has begun to flow with her moon cycle.

The room of the celebration can be decorated with flowers preferably red and white. A chalice of juice and some red fruit and cakes with red or pink icing is on the altar. The beginning of the celebration should be a relaxing time of the women making a fuss of her, giving feminine gifts wrapped in red tissue or wrapping paper. Someone could give her a foot massage or do her hair, perhaps give her a facial. It's an afternoon or evening of women's pleasures, but she is the focus of it.

The actual ceremony is quite simple. The women form a circle. If her girl friends have begun their periods they can join the circle. If not, they must sit outside of the circle and wait till the end. The girl's Mother leaves the circle and leads her daughter to the edge. The oldest woman there who will represent the Crone aspect of the Goddess says;

"Who is it that seeks entrance to the circle of Woman and why do you come?"

The Girls Mother says - "This is my daughter, born of my blood. She has become a woman and seeks to know the mysteries"

The Crone now says "What do you bring, as proof, to join this circle of Woman?"

The Girl steps forward and hands the Crone either a red ribbon, or if she wishes, she can have earlier prepared a small piece of cotton or muslin, stained with some of her own blood. The Crone takes the token and smiling says "Leave your childhood and enter as a Woman - may you be blessed and learn all from the circle of women".

She is brought into the circle and all the women kiss and hug her.

Her Mother will bless the chalice and the daughter must bless the cakes and serve the circle of women. Then each woman will give her a 'piece of advice' or share something of her wisdom. Afterwards, the circle disbands and the food is shared.

Requiem

Having touched briefly on the subject of death with the Samhain festival, there are going to be times in your family's lives when there is the loss of family members, friends or even family pets. As Pagans we (hopefully) don't fear the end of our physical lives believing in some kind of reincarnation, and not having a fear of being in an eternal fire if we haven't been 'saved' by christianity. Children do see this in different ways often depending on their ages and what ideas they have been exposed to in their lives so far. It seems to be quite normal for children to be farmed out with relatives rather than attending the funerals of their family, but apart from young children that may be a distraction, I don't think this is a good thing. We need to get rid of the attitude of hiding death from children; it is after all, a completely normal experience for all of us eventually in our lives.

However the feelings of the bereaved are most important at this time, and if they prefer your children to be absent from the funeral rite, you may need to have your own requiem ceremony at home to allow the children to say goodbye if they wish. Obviously this is more likely with pets as far as children are concerned, but still this is good experience for them.

Some Pagans will have different ideas for burial and funeral rites, there are lots of natural burial sites springing up around the countryside where the funeral is an eco-affair with cardboard coffins and the deceased having a tree planted on their grave. Crematoriums are far more open to different kinds of funerals and will happily accommodate your different ideas.

If a person close to your family has died and your child wants to do something to say goodbye, but the bereaved do not want children at the funeral, then you could either have a formal ceremony in the circle at home, or you can do something more informal - perhaps make something (that will decompose) or take some flowers out on a nature walk. There you can remember the person together and celebrate them before leaving the offering by a tree or other useful place. They can also be remembered at the next Samhain festival if you wish.

For a slightly more formal ceremony I would have the circle on the same day as the funeral is planned if this is possible. The altar is decorated with whatever greenery or flowers are appropriate for that time of year, taking into account any personal associations of the deceased. If it is a pet, something to symbolise it may be used; perhaps some of its personal items like feeding bowl or favourite toy. There is one lit black and one unlit white candle in the centre. A chalice of juice and a dish of oatcakes, which represents grain from the earth to which we all return.

We open the circle and sit together in the middle to think about the one we have lost for a few moments. Then I will invite people to share things they would like to say, events they remember and other special memories of them. Sometimes there will be laughter and there may also be tears. (It's a good idea to have a box of tissues in the circle just in case). We will talk about what happens to us when we die and I will share my feelings and beliefs on reincarnation and what is now a time of rest before the next experiences of life begins. We may sing the chant 'we all come from the Goddess' mentioned in an earlier chapter, or an elemental chant - 'The earth, the air, the fire, the water, return, return, return'. We will bless a chalice of juice and the oatcakes and share them - making a toast and a blessing as we pass the cup.

Finally when we have said all we need, laughed or cried as much as we can in this time, we go to the altar and say ' It was good to know you and will be good to know you again - Merry meet, merry part and merry meet again' All of us will blow out the black candle together. Then we light the white candle saying 'May this light the way on your journey forwards'. The circle is closed, we share food and drink and the white candle is put somewhere safe to burn down without extinguishing it. (the safest place - especially if its possible it may burn all night is in a glass bowl, which is placed in another larger bowl of water in the kitchen sink!).

Chapter Seven

Blessings, Chants and Prayers

These are some daily blessings from the family book. They are not great poetry - just something that has meaning to our family. We may not do these blessings every day, although I try to include a blessing on our mealtimes at least once a day. I will usually include them on special occasions - perhaps on a season festival or on the day of a full moon.

Please feel free to use them yourselves if you wish, or even better - make up your own ones and personalise them - it will mean so much more to you and your family.

Morning Blessing

Bless our day that lies before us
May we be creative, loving and thankful
For all the abundance we receive
Blessed Be

Blessing Before Dinner

We thank our Mother Earth for the food before us
And may we always remember from
Whence it comes
Blessed Be

Evening Blessing

Thank you for all the games and the fun
Thank you for everything that we have done
Bless us as we sleep tonight
Safely to the morning light
Blessed Be

Family Totems and Chants

All families have a family or clan totem and it is easy to find out what it is. A meditational journey to the underworld using whatever method you prefer to reach it - possibly a cave or passage that leads to an underground temple. My journey to find our family totem found me in an underworld temple with the roots of a great tree coming out of the roof. With a large club I found there I beat the roots like a drum until the being or animal would come and claim our family as our totem guide.

My family totem at present is a crow, although there can be individual ones for each family member too, and sometimes the totem can change for a variety of reasons.

We have a chant to the crow to welcome it to be part of our family ceremonines and special meals.

Chant to the Crow

Ancient One of Land and Sky,
Be our eyes and strength to see.
Let us live and learn to fly.
Teach us your wisdom and how to be free.

Prayer to the Goddess

This is my own prayer to the Goddess I use every night when I put my little girl to bed. She usually has a milky drink and a cuddle before being tucked in, and it is nice to say this prayer while we cuddle.

May the Goddess surround you and protect you and keep you
safe
May She give you a good night's sleep with peaceful dreams
May you be warm and cozy as you sleep - not too hot or cold
May you sleep with no disturbances or distractions until
morning.

May our home always be filled with love and light
That nothing else may enter.
May we always be surrounded by good friends and
neighbours
May our lives be filled with abundance and prosperity and
May we always remember to give thanks for what we have
And share it with others
May we have long lives and good health
May we be tolerant and patient
And may our lives be filled with joy, love and laughter
Blessed Be

Endnote

There are other celebrations that families will do together - handfasting is always enjoyable with children taking part, especially if they have a task such as throwing the petals before the couple, or holding the rings or the sword. You may want to honour a Crone in the family or Coven with a special circle.

There may be a time when you want to do some healing or other magical work where you feel that your children would also benefit from being there. I decided to leave out such things as I didn't feel it fitted with my idea of what this book is about. It is written as a guide to celebrating family and nature with the children being the central part in the celebrations - not as guests of someone else's party. As I said earlier, this is my own way of doing things and is not given to you as the only way of celebrating life, but I offer it to you as some ideas and activities that I know my family and friends have enjoyed and hope you enjoy taking part in, and celebrating with, your children.

Appendix 1 - useful addresses and further reading

The Woodcraft Folk
13 Ritherdon Road
London SW17 8QE
Email;info@woodcraft.org.uk

The Pagan Federation (SAE)
BM Box 7097
London WC1N 3XX
Email;secretary@Paganfed.org

Education Otherwise
PO box 7420
London N9 9SG
Net;www.education-otherwise.org

The Green Parent Magazine
PO Box 104
Lewes BN7 9AX
Net;www.thegreenparent.co.uk

Further Reading;

A Calendar of Festivals by Marion Green

Pagan Feasts - seasonal food for the Eight Festivals by Anna Franklin and Sue Phillips

Festivals family and food by Diana Carey and Judy Large

Earthwise - Environmental crafts and activities with young children

The Green Parent often has interesting seasonal articles.

Appendix 2 - Astrology notes for classroom presentation

These are my notes for a short talk that I did for my son's school class when he was eight years old. You may find them useful for discussing with your family.

Astrology

The science of Astrology began many thousands of years ago. It was a science of omens. People thought that two planets passing close together might mean something was coming - like a famine, or perhaps a flood. The people who did this began to chart the position of the stars and the planets they knew about to create this science. It grew to becoming a very complicated system used to answer all sorts of questions.

The rules we use today are the same ones laid down in Babylon over 4,000 years ago. Until the early 1700's mathematicians, soldiers, politicians, doctors and other professionals used it for their work. About 300 years ago it stopped being a science and was mainly used for personal reasons. Astrology is like a fingerprint. Everyone has something different, even if it's only a very small difference, no one chart is ever the same as someone else's.

Astrology is often called the study of symbols and cycles. Symbols because the planets represent parts of your life -

events and happenings. Cycles, because each planet has a cycle of movement it goes through around the sun, and so do our lives and the things that affect us - weather, birthdays, seasons and so on.

The symbols are a kind of code for things we find difficult to explain in words. Like our hopes and dreams or fears. Things we may feel but can't express.

Astrology is full of Gods. Greek, Roman, Mesopotamian and Babylonian. These are Archetypes - that is they are forces that represent bits of our personality and characters.

Although the Sun is actually a Star, and the Moon is a Satellite of the Earth, they are still called planets in Astrology because the Greeks used the work Planet to mean 'Heavenly Wanderer'. That includes all the planets and stars really, but we tend to keep to the ones we know.

Each of the planets rules a variety of different things. There are special charts listing these called 'tables of correspondences. We don't need to remember everything on these, just to try and form a picture of the personality of each planet will help you to understand them a bit more.

Up until 1781, people thought there were only 7 planets until a man called Herschel discovered Uranus. Then in 1846 Neptune was discovered. In 1930 it was the turn of Pluto and then in 1974 another one was seen. It was called Chiron and is supposed to be special for Healing. (since this talk was written another planet has been discovered recently - given the name of Sedna).

Now if we think of the personality of the planets, we can see how they might be people you know or even recognise in yourself. Close your eyes for a moment and imagine these people as I describe them.

The Sun - The sun is a friendly sunny little boy. He might also be a king. The King of the day. He isn't trying to pretend to be grown up or important. He likes to laugh and play. The sun usually means how you react to life and what you might like to get out of it.

The Moon - The moon is the Queen of the night. Imagine her sitting on a throne of silver. She may have a baby on her lap too. She could be in a boat or ship - a bit like an Egyptian barge, on a deep, calm sea. The moon usually means how you feel. Your emotions. How you might long for things too. She is a very motherly figure.

Mercury - Think of an young man who might like to play tricks. Or he likes to do puzzles and think up new ideas. He is really good at understanding computers and how they work or doing mathematics. When you need to use a dictionary or thesaurus he can help you with it. Mercury describes how your mind works. Your attitudes to information and how you communicate with people.

Venus - Venus is usually a very beautiful woman. Sometimes she likes to sit in a lovely garden full of flowers with wonderful smells. She looks like a famous pop-star or film actress. Everyone falls in love with her. She paints pictures and writes poetry and loves going out with her boyfriend. Venus describes what things you might be attracted to. The way you feel about other people in your life, or they feel about you. And your creative or artistic interests.

Mars - This is when I think of a warrior. It could be a Viking with a double axe or a Knight with a heavy broadsword. Perhaps an American Indian brave with a leathery face, or even a modern day soldier. He might be very loud and brash, getting angry easily. He makes lots of noise and loves a good fight. He knows what he wants and will try and get it even if he has to battle for it. Mars usually means your determination and the things you really want. It is your ambition and success but can also mean your temper!

Jupiter - he is a jolly, fat uncle who likes to give you treats. He always has a bag of sweets in his pocket and brings a cake when he visits. He looks for the best in people and is likely to play the lottery (he'd probably win it too!). Jupiter describes your optimistic thoughts. Your luck and opportunities. He likes to reach further than people thought he could, he has lots of fun and enjoys everything he does.

Saturn - Saturn is an old mysterious figure. Usually a man, although it can also be a withered old woman too. Saturn wears a dark cloak with a hood and walks very slowly. When you don't want to do your bedroom out or homework before you go out to play, Saturn will make you sit down and finish it first. Saturn describes your fears and barriers. It puts limits on some activities and provides discipline and authority.

Uranus - This is a man who rushes around changing things he doesn't like. He loves new things and doesn't want to stay the same for too long. He will probably start new fashions and design clothes or houses and he loves new technology. He'll say things like "you cannot stop progress". This is to do with your own changes and how you react to them - especially if they are dramatic ones.

Neptune - This is an absent-minded professor. He walks around with glasses on the end of his nose and may specialise in the science of the mind as a psychologist. He likes taking photos and going to the cinema. He likes hidden thoughts and thinks very deeply about the meaning of life. Neptune has a special influence on your deep mind and your reaction to inventions or discoveries.

Pluto - Pluto is a very powerful man. Be may be an investment banker or work in stocks and shares. A leader of a government or even a king. He doesn't tend to be very wise though. He tends to make things a bit difficult for people, doesn't care if he takes your home and money and leaves you poor. If he wants to build a road and your house is in the way, he will knock it down without worrying where you will go. He may also be a scientist that experiments without caring if what he does is right or not.

In astrology we work out people's charts from the time and place they were born by looking at where the planets were in the sky at that time. It's a bit like a map with sections called HOUSES that symbolise certain times in your life - like the time of your education or what kind of work you may do. The astrologer will find out your Sun and Moon signs. The sun sign is what people use for reading their horoscopes in magazines and papers. This one refers to the date and month you were born and is your potential - what you might become. We look at the place and time you were born for the Moon sign. This is the dreamy side of you. Special charts called an Ephemeris are used to work it out.

Finally we work out the longitude and latitude of the place you were born. You can find this on a globe or in an atlas. This gives you your ASCENDANT sign. This is your main personality. We use the Ephemeris again and from this we can work out your chart and find out where all the other planets were at the moment of your birth and what HOUSE they were in and what effect they may have on your personality. This is a map of you at your birth.

Now each sign is ruled by an ELEMENT. Earth, Air, Fire and Water. We are made up of all of these elements and each sign is ruled by one of them so may have a greater effect on you.

Earth - rules our practical selves and down to earth nature. Our physical bodies and everyday life like money and your home.

Earth rules TAURUS, VIRGO AND CAPRICORN

Air - rules our thoughts and ideas and mental processes. And what we say.

Air rules GEMINI, LIBRA AND AQUARIUS

Fire - rules our will power and energy. Determination and enthusiasm

Fire rules ARIES, LEO AND SAGITTARIUS

Water - rules our emotions and dreams and our religious or spiritual feelings

Water rules CANCER, SCORPIO AND PISCES.

The first sign of the Zodiac is Aries then followed by Taurus, Gemini, Cancer, Leo, Virgo, Libra, Scorpio, Sagittarius, Capricorn, Aquarius and Pisces.

The signs each run from about the 21st of each month although depending on the Ephemeris they can run a day or two later. This will be known as 'being on the cusp' when you could have some of either sign for your sun sign. This is why we need a date and time and place for your birth. Using this information we can draw up a fairly accurate idea of the personality you have. However, you can change things about yourself if you don't like what your chart says about you. It's just a starting off point.

You may find these Capall Bann titles of interest:

Let Your Children Go Back To Nature John Hodgson & Alan Dyer

'Its a book and an idea and an educational at a deep and true level' The Times Educational Supplement.

This ground-breaking book by two long-experienced educationalists offers parents and teachers an attractive means to ameliorate the deadening demands of the National Curriculum. It is crammed with new and stimulating ideas, games and creative activities that have already delighted thousands of children of all abilities. The ideas and adventures in this book started as a two year experiment with 24 Devon children; the concept proved so popular that is grew to encompass many more activities and thousands of children across southern England. The aim is to provide not only enjoyment, but also 'real' education - strongly reinforced by direct experience, games and creative activities. Activities include story-telling, costumes, poetry, music and dances, drama, games for fun and enchantment, traditional country activities, and much more - an 'Enchanters' Brew' of ideas and activities with plenty of nourishment for young minds and bodies - for the children *and* you! ISBN 186163 1723   £12.95

Celebrating Nature   Gordon MacLellan

A practical handbook of celebration. For a small youth group, a family or a gathering of several hundred people, this book offers guidelines and a range of ideas for designing and leading celebrations that will grow from people's own imaginations. Activities are generally short and might stand alone as small celebrations in themselves or can be combined to create longer and more spectacular events. A number of ways of exploring the natural world and the sorts of celebrations that might arise from these adventures are presented. Different structures for celebrations are described and how to make the most of the enthusiasm and creativity of the participants. The many topics covered include: The importance of celebration; Historical celebrations and their survival into current times; Celebrations as ways of sharing experiences; Principles and activities to use in finding ideas; Inspiring a group; Personal celebrations; Working with natural materials; Working with stories; Developing storytelling skills; Animated Trails: an application of story work: creating performance pieces: activities include puppets, twig people, foam toadstools, and more. Plotting and planning a trail with a group; Activities for making and working with flags, banners, standards. Planning and leading a procession, Working with music; Performance and presentation skills: movement activities for puppets, masks and costumes, working with the spoken word, telling stories, creating characters; Working with groups of people of various sizes and minimal equipment: mumming plays, instant meditations, leading dances; Behind the scenes planning; Putting it all together: structures of celebrations: atmosphere and activity, mapping out a whole celebration, managing your participants, keeping people involved, practical tips. An immensely practical, inspiring book for everyone - another masterly work from Gordon the Toad!
ISBN 186163 1685   £14.95

FREE DETAILED
CATALOGUE

Capall Bann is owned and run by people actively involved in many of the areas in which we publish. A detailed illustrated catalogue is available on request, SAE or International Postal Coupon appreciated. **Titles can be ordered direct from Capall Bann, post free in the UK** (cheque or PO with order) or from good bookshops and specialist outlets.

A Breath Behind Time, Terri Hector
A Soul is Born by Eleyna Williamson
Angels and Goddesses - Celtic Christianity & Paganism, M. Howard
The Art of Conversation With the Genius Loci, Barry Patterson
Arthur - The Legend Unveiled, C Johnson & E Lung
Astrology The Inner Eye - A Guide in Everyday Language, E Smith
Auguries and Omens - The Magical Lore of Birds, Yvonne Aburrow
Asyniur - Women's Mysteries in the Northern Tradition, S McGrath
Beginnings - Geomancy, Builder's Rites & Electional Astrology in the
    European Tradition, Nigel Pennick
Between Earth and Sky, Julia Day
Book of the Veil , Peter Paddon
The Book of Seidr, Runic John
Caer Sidhe - Celtic Astrology and Astronomy, Michael Bayley
Call of the Horned Piper, Nigel Jackson
Can't Sleep, Won't Sleep, Linda Louisa Dell
Carnival of the Animals, Gregor Lamb
Cat's Company, Ann Walker
Celebrating Nature, Gordon MacLellan
Celtic Faery Shamanism, Catrin James
Celtic Faery Shamanism - The Wisdom of the Otherworld, Catrin James
Celtic Lore & Druidic Ritual, Rhiannon Ryall
Celtic Sacrifice - Pre Christian Ritual & Religion, Marion Pearce
Celtic Saints and the Glastonbury Zodiac, Mary Caine
Circle and the Square, Jack Gale
Come Back To Life, Jenny Smedley
Company of Heaven, Jan McDonald
Compleat Vampyre - The Vampyre Shaman, Nigel Jackson
Cottage Witchcraft, Jan McDonald
Creating Form From the Mist - The Wisdom of Women in Celtic Myth and
    Culture, Lynne Sinclair-Wood
Crystal Clear - A Guide to Quartz Crystal, Jennifer Dent
Crystal Doorways, Simon & Sue Lilly

Crossing the Borderlines - Guising, Masking & Ritual Animal Disguise in the
European Tradition, Nigel Pennick
Dragons of the West, Nigel Pennick
Earth Dance - A Year of Pagan Rituals, Jan Brodie
Earth Harmony - Places of Power, Holiness & Healing, Nigel Pennick
Earth Magic, Margaret McArthur
Egyptian Animals - Guardians & Gateways of the Gods, Akkadia Ford
Eildon Tree (The) Romany Language & Lore, Michael Hoadley
Enchanted Forest - The Magical Lore of Trees, Yvonne Aburrow
Eternal Priestess, Sage Weston
Eternally Yours Faithfully, Roy Radford & Evelyn Gregory
Everything You Always Wanted To Know About Your Body, But So Far
Nobody's Been Able To Tell You, Chris Thomas & D Baker
Experiencing the Green Man, Rob Hardy & Teresa Moorey
Face of the Deep - Healing Body & Soul, Penny Allen
Fairies and Nature Spirits, Teresa Moorey
Fairies in the Irish Tradition, Molly Gowen
Familiars - Animal Powers of Britain, Anna Franklin
Flower Wisdom, Katherine Kear
Fool's First Steps, (The) Chris Thomas
Forest Paths - Tree Divination, Brian Harrison, Ill. S. Rouse
From Past to Future Life, Dr Roger Webber
From Stagecraft To Witchcraft, , Patricia Crowther
Gardening For Wildlife Ron Wilson
God Year, The, Nigel Pennick & Helen Field
Goddess on the Cross, Dr George Young
Goddess Year, The, Nigel Pennick & Helen Field
Goddesses, Guardians & Groves, Jack Gale
Handbook For Pagan Healers, Liz Joan
Handbook of Fairies, Ronan Coghlan
Healing Book, The, Chris Thomas and Diane Baker
Healing Homes, Jennifer Dent
Healing Journeys, Paul Williamson
Healing Stones, Sue Philips
Herb Craft - Shamanic & Ritual Use of Herbs, Lavender & Franklin
Hidden Heritage - Exploring Ancient Essex, Terry Johnson
Hub of the Wheel, Skytoucher
In and Out the Windows, Dilys Gator
In Search of Herne the Hunter, Eric Fitch
In Search of the Green Man, Peter Hill
Inner Celtia, Alan Richardson & David Annwn
Inner Mysteries of the Goths, Nigel Pennick
Inner Space Workbook - Develop Through Tarot, Cat Summers & Julian Vayne
In Search of Pagan Gods, Teresa Moorey
Intuitive Journey, Ann Walker Isis - African Queen, Akkadia Ford
Journey Home, The, Chris Thomas

Kecks, Keddles & Kesh - Celtic Lang & The Cog Almanac, Bayley
Language of the Psycards, Berenice
Legend of Robin Hood, The, Richard Rutherford-Moore
Lid Off the Cauldron, Patricia Crowther
Light From the Shadows - Modern Traditional Witchcraft, Gwyn
Living Tarot, Ann Walker
Lore of the Sacred Horse, Marion Davies
Lost Lands & Sunken Cities (2nd ed.), Nigel Pennick
The Magic and Mystery of Trees, Teresa Moorey
Magic For the Next 1,000 Years, Jack Gale
Magic of Herbs - A Complete Home Herbal, Rhiannon Ryall
Magical Guardians - Exploring the Spirit and Nature of Trees, Philip Heselton
Magical History of the Horse, Janet Farrar & Virginia Russell
Magical Lore of Animals, Yvonne Aburrow
Magical Lore of Cats, Marion Davies
Magical Lore of Herbs, Marion Davies
Magick Without Peers, Ariadne Rainbird & David Rankine
Masks of Misrule - Horned God & His Cult in Europe, Nigel Jackson
Medicine For The Coming Age, Lisa Sand MD
Medium Rare - Reminiscences of a Clairvoyant, Muriel Renard
Menopausal Woman on the Run, Jaki da Costa
Mind Massage - 60 Creative Visualisations, Marlene Maundrill
Mirrors of Magic - Evoking the Spirit of the Dewponds, P Heselton
The Moon and You, Teresa Moorey
Moon Mysteries, Jan Brodie
Mysteries of the Runes, Michael Howard
Mystic Life of Animals, Ann Walker
New Celtic Oracle The, Nigel Pennick & Nigel Jackson
Oracle of Geomancy, Nigel Pennick
Pagan Feasts - Seasonal Food for the 8 Festivals, Franklin & Phillips
Paganism For Teens, Jess Wynne
Patchwork of Magic - Living in a Pagan World, Julia Day
Pathworking - A Practical Book of Guided Meditations, Pete Jennings
Personal Power, Anna Franklin
Pickingill Papers - The Origins of Gardnerian Wicca, Bill Liddell
Pillars of Tubal Cain, Nigel Jackson
Places of Pilgrimage and Healing, Adrian Cooper
Planet Earth - The Universe's Experiment, Chris Thomas
Practical Divining, Richard Foord
Practical Meditation, Steve Hounsome
Practical Spirituality, Steve Hounsome
Psychic Self Defence - Real Solutions, Jan Brodie
Real Fairies, David Tame
Reality - How It Works & Why It Mostly Doesn't, Rik Dent
Romany Tapestry, Michael Houghton
Runic Astrology, Nigel Pennick

Sacred Animals, Gordon MacLellan
Sacred Celtic Animals, Marion Davies, Ill. Simon Rouse
Sacred Dorset - On the Path of the Dragon, Peter Knight
Sacred Grove - The Mysteries of the Forest, Yvonne Aburrow
Sacred Geometry, Nigel Pennick
Sacred Nature, Ancient Wisdom & Modern Meanings, A Cooper
Sacred Ring - Pagan Origins of British Folk Festivals, M. Howard
Season of Sorcery - On Becoming a Wisewoman, Poppy Palin
Seasonal Magic - Diary of a Village Witch, Paddy Slade
Secret Places of the Goddess, Philip Heselton
Secret Signs & Sigils, Nigel Pennick
The Secrets of East Anglian Magic, Nigel Pennick
A Seeker's Guide To Past Lives, Paul Williamson
Seeking Pagan Gods, Teresa Moorey
A Seer's Guide To Crystal Divination, Gale Halloran
Self Enlightenment, Mayan O'Brien
Soul Resurgence, Poppy Palin
Spirits of the Air, Jaq D Hawkins
Spirits of the Water, Jaq D Hawkins
Spirits of the Fire, Jaq D Hawkins
Spirits of the Aether, Jaq D Hawkins
Spirits of the Earth, Jaq D Hawkins
Stony Gaze, Investigating Celtic Heads John Billingsley
Stumbling Through the Undergrowth , Mark Kirwan-Heyhoe
Subterranean Kingdom, The, revised 2nd ed, Nigel Pennick
Symbols of Ancient Gods, Rhiannon Ryall
Talking to the Earth, Gordon MacLellan
Talking With Nature, Julie Hood
Taming the Wolf - Full Moon Meditations, Steve Hounsome
Teachings of the Wisewomen, Rhiannon Ryall
The Other Kingdoms Speak, Helena Hawley
Transformation of Housework, Ben Bushill
Tree: Essence of Healing, Simon & Sue Lilly
Tree: Essence, Spirit & Teacher, Simon & Sue Lilly
Tree Seer, Simon & Sue Lilly
Through the Veil, Peter Paddon
Torch and the Spear, Patrick Regan
Understanding Chaos Magic, Jaq D Hawkins
Understanding Past Lives, Dilys Gater
Understanding Second Sight, Dilys Gater
Understanding Spirit Guides, Dilys Gater
Understanding Star Children, Dilys Gater
The Urban Shaman, Dilys Gater
Vortex - The End of History, Mary Russell
Warp and Weft - In Search of the I-Ching, William de Fancourt
Warriors at the Edge of Time, Jan Fry

Water Witches, Tony Steele
Way of the Magus, Michael Howard
Weaving a Web of Magic, Rhiannon Ryall
West Country Wicca, Rhiannon Ryall
What's Your Poison? vol 1, Tina Tarrant
Wheel of the Year, Teresa Moorey & Jane Brideson
Wildwitch - The Craft of the Natural Psychic, Poppy Palin
Wildwood King , Philip Kane
A Wisewoman's Book of Tea Leaf Reading, Pat Barki
The Witching Path, Moira Stirland
The Witch's Kitchen, Val Thomas
The Witches' Heart, Eileen Smith
Witches of Oz, Matthew & Julia Philips
Witchcraft Myth Magic Mystery and... Not Forgetting Fairies, Ralph Harvey
Wondrous Land - The Faery Faith of Ireland by Dr Kay Mullin
Working With Crystals, Shirley o'Donoghue
Working With Natural Energy, Shirley o'Donoghue
Working With the Merlin, Geoff Hughes
Your Talking Pet, Ann Walker
The Zodiac Experience, Patricia Crowther

FREE detailed catalogue and FREE 'Inspiration' magazine

Contact: Capall Bann Publishing, Auton Farm, Milverton, Somerset, TA4 1NE